OUTSIDE MY WINDOW

UNDERSTANDING CHILDREN AND
THE STRESS/TRAUMA RESPONSE MODEL

WRITTEN BY
VICKY SCOTT
ILLUSTRATED BY
JACQUI GIBBS CHAMBERLAIN

LIFE CO BOOKS

Vicky Scott, RN, BA, MAHons Psych, PGDip Psych Practice, is a Registered Psychologist and provider of psychological services for Accident Compensation Corporation, the Ministry for Children Oranga Tamariki, and the New Zealand Defence Force. She has a clinical and theoretical interest in complex trauma, and transpersonal psychology. Vicky is a mother and grandmother and lives with her partner David and their dog Frankie in Whanganui, where she maintains her clinical practice, focused primarily on the treatment of child, youth and adult trauma. Her other passions are family and travel. Email: vicky@lifeco-psychology.co.nz

Jacqui Gibbs Chamberlain is an artist of figurative subjects. She has travelled widely, to the US for workshops, and to Papua New Guinea, China, India and Samoa. She has also lived in Switzerland and spent time painting in the Outback of Australia. Jacqui is a previous recipient of the Designer's Institute CoCA Award. Her main subject matter is the human figure, but her work also explores shape, form and composition. She lives on an isolated farm in Port Levy, Banks Peninsula, with her husband and daughter. Email: jgibbschamberlain@xtra.co.nz

First published in 2019 by LifeCo Books
An imprint of LifeCo Psychology Ltd
142 Springvale Road, Whanganui 4509, New Zealand
www.lifeco-psychology.co.nz

First published 2019

ISBN 978-0-473-48268-8

Also available as an e-book

A catalogue record for this book is available from the National Library of New Zealand.

Project management: Linda Cassells, Calico Publishing
Cover and typesetting: Julie McDermid, Punaromia Publications
Brain illustration on page 63 and WOT graphics by Deborah Hinde

To all the children, young people and adults
who have shared their experiences of trauma
and given a voice to the little person inside
who has been struggling to survive.
You are so brave.

Introduction

Children who have adverse life experiences are often judged by their behaviour or may be labelled with diagnoses. They are often in survival mode because of their traumatic experiences. *Outside My Window* helps readers to understand what happens in survival mode, or as one little person said, 'I am not bad … just sad and mad'.

The purpose of this book is to teach young children primarily aged 5–12, their carers, teachers and therapists about the impact of Adverse Childhood Experiences (ACEs) on their feelings, body, behaviour and thoughts about themselves.

Vicky's practice is based on the premise that 'we do the best we can with the tools we have at the time'. Children (and later adults) who are dealing with family violence in all its forms, and/or neglect, do not have the skills and resources to cope with such experiences. Survival mode is the natural strategy, and it may continue to be used well into adult life.

Outside My Window is based on the 'Window Of Tolerance' (WOT) model of autonomic arousal, which was first put forward by Dr Daniel Siegel in 1999. In this stress/trauma response model he proposed that between the extremes of sympathetic hyperarousal and para-sympathetic hypoarousal is a 'window' or range of optimal arousal states in which emotions can be experienced as tolerable and are therefore able to be integrated.

Educating parents, teachers, caregivers, and those who work with children, youth and traumatised adults about the stress model allows for therapeutic, compassionate and helpful conversations that remove blame and shame. There is less judgement, more cooperation, and greater safety for a child who is outside their window.

A note for carers, counsellors, parents and teachers

The stress/trauma response model helps to identify risks, enabling the child to recognise their survival response without feeling there is something intrinsically wrong with them. A conversation can take place that gives a child permission to talk about their fears and worries so that support can be implemented.

The model can be used on a whiteboard for therapeutic assessment and psycho-education, enabling information-gathering without the child feeling that they are the sole focus of attention, which could otherwise result in shut-down. Problems are seen within a global human framework, rather than as personal behaviour issues.

As you read *Outside My Window* with children, use it as an opportunity to have a conversation about safety and concerns, and seek support or notify services if at any time a child reports any of the worries dealt with in this book.

Outside My Window is also used with traumatised adults as they often have a hurt child part inside who can relate to and has experienced the trauma/survival response. It has often brought tears and relief.

I have a window
you can't really see.

It's inside
my brain and
looks after me.

Inside my window it's a gentle, wavy ride.

My moods come and go,

like riding on a slide.

Some days are happy,

and some days are sad.

Some days
are good,
and some days
are bad.

It's called my 'window of tolerance',
or the WOT.

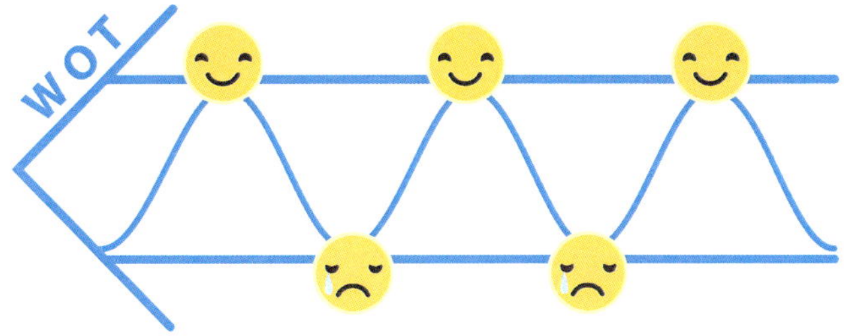

It's how many worries
I can hold
and still behave
like I'm me.

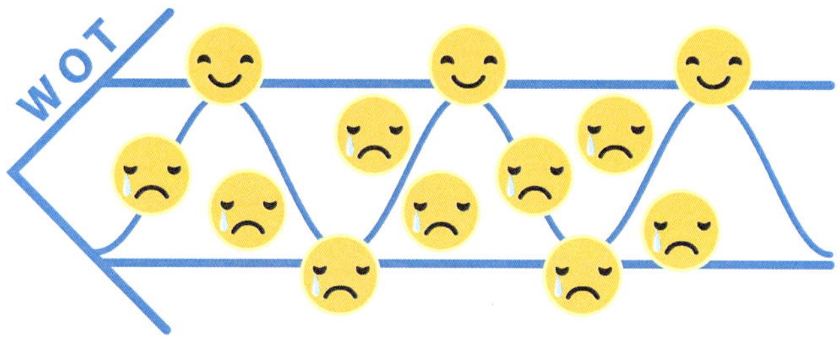

Worries like doing well at school,
or friends liking me,

Some tricky maths,
a little cough,
a scratch on
my knee.

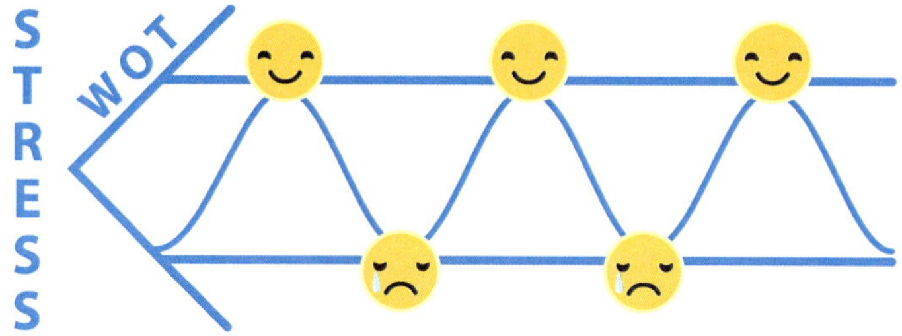

Gentle ride worries -
they're just
everyday stress.

But choppy ride worries mean

my window's in a mess.

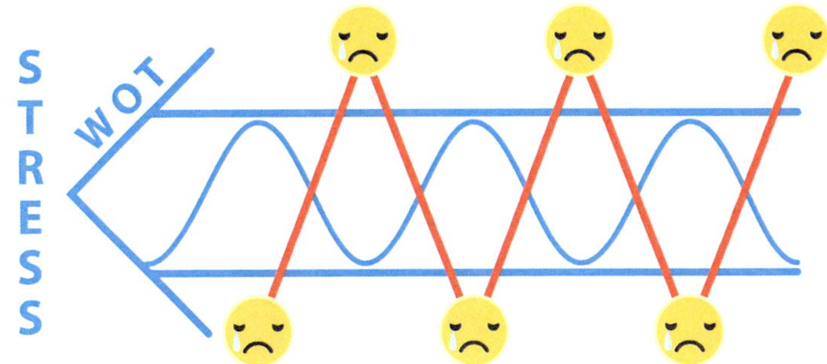

Choppy rides tell my brain
it's important to be ready.

I'm in for a real rough ride.
Things are now unsteady!

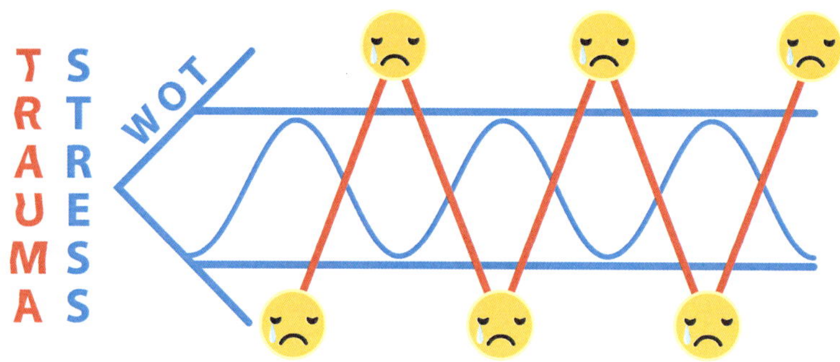

Trauma is what we call it
when there's way too much stress.

It sends a message to my brain
to do what it does best.

Three brains
inside my head,
all work together.

They kick into play

when it's really
stormy weather.

There's the Mammal Brain,
Reptile Brain,
Human Brain - and
my Amygdala Pea.

I'm now outside
my window
and can't be
my best me.

The Pea tells my Mammal Brain,
'It's FIGHT or FLIGHT or FREEZE.'

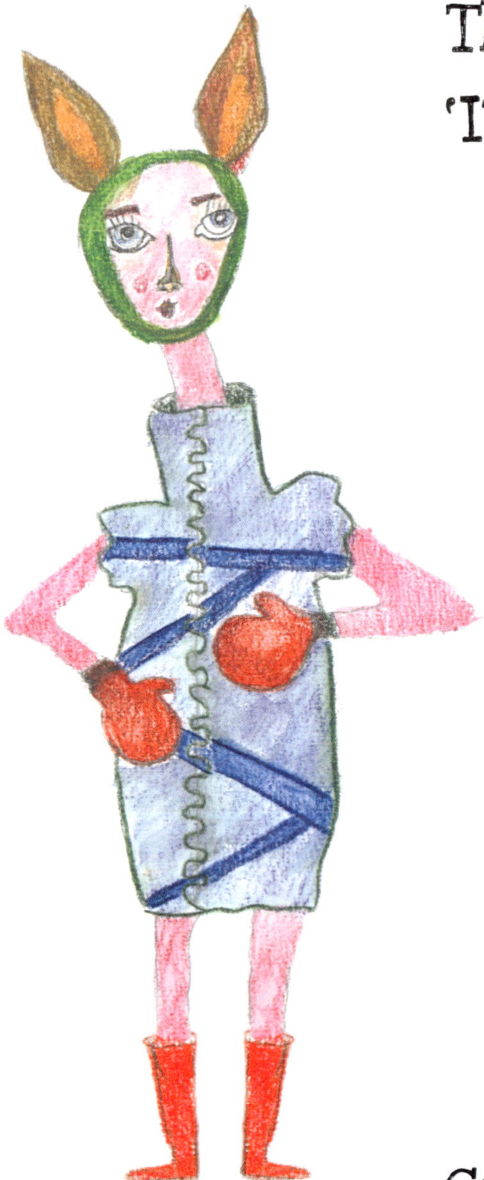

Grown-ups think I'm naughty
when I'm stuck in one of these.

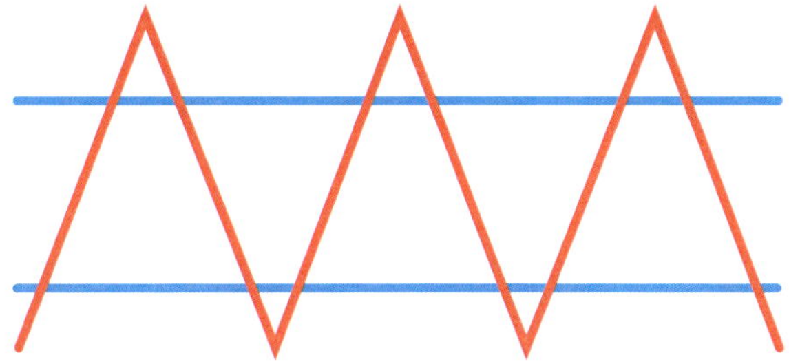

If I come out in FIGHT,
I'm angry
and I ROAR.

I fight with friends and argue back,

and slam the classroom door.

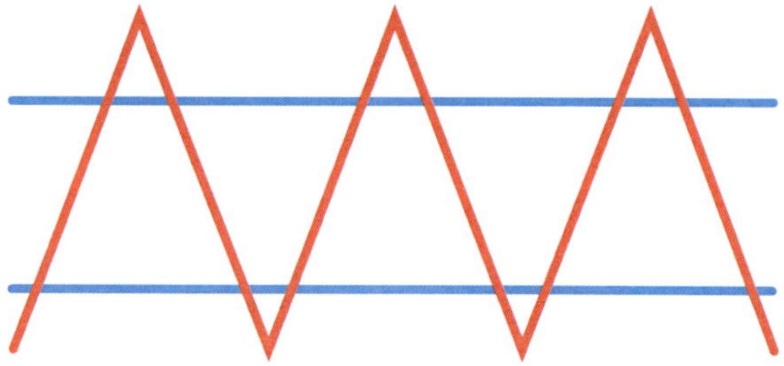

If I come out in FLIGHT
I have to race to get away.

I take off from the ones I love,
I can't concentrate or play.

If I FREEZE,
my body's still,

but my mind is
in a race.

I worry about all the awful things.

For me there's no safe place.

If I stay outside
my window
for too long a time,

Reptile Brain comes in to help
and gives Mammal Brain a sign.

'Take a rest.
It's way too hard.
You really tried and tried.

FIGHT-FLIGHT-FREEZE
is not enough.
Now it's time to hide.'

I go to bed

with the covers

over my head ...

At school I find a cupboard,
or crawl under a desk.

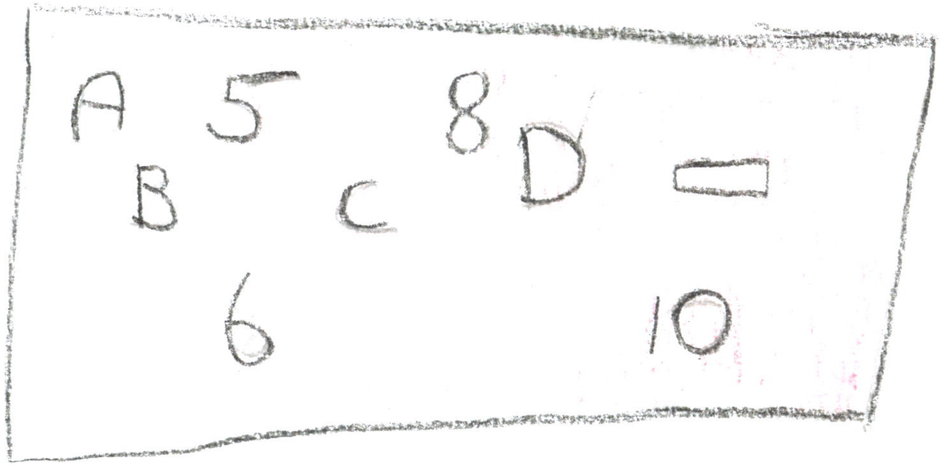

Shutting down
and closing off
is what the
Reptile Brain
does best.

'So what about the Human Brain?'
I thought you'd never ask!

The Human Brain
just switches off.
It simply wears
a mask.

At school, you can tell
it isn't really me,
'cos 'outside my window'
can look like ADHD.

Attention Deficit Hyperactivity Disorder
school ABC
HELP

I can't focus on my school work.

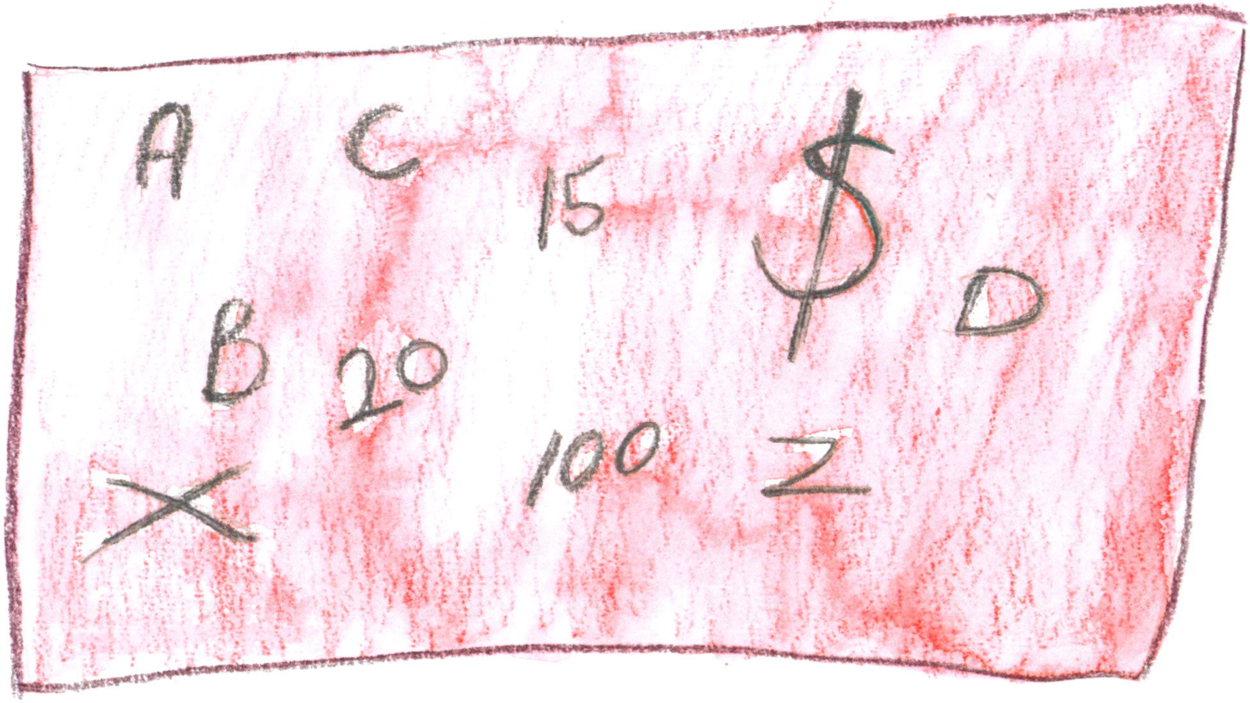

It's like my brain's asleep.

I shout and yell at everyone,

or I don't make a peep.

My head hurts,
my tummy hurts,
I don't know
what to do.

It's my cry for help,
my DANGER ZONE.
I'm calling out to you.

Please ask me,
'Am I safe at home
or school?
Is everything OK?

Is there someone hurting me, something I'm afraid to say?'

It can really make a difference
when you can see my WOT.

I won't get hurt, misplaced or lost
If you keep your eye on me.

This is what it's like when I am outside my WOT:

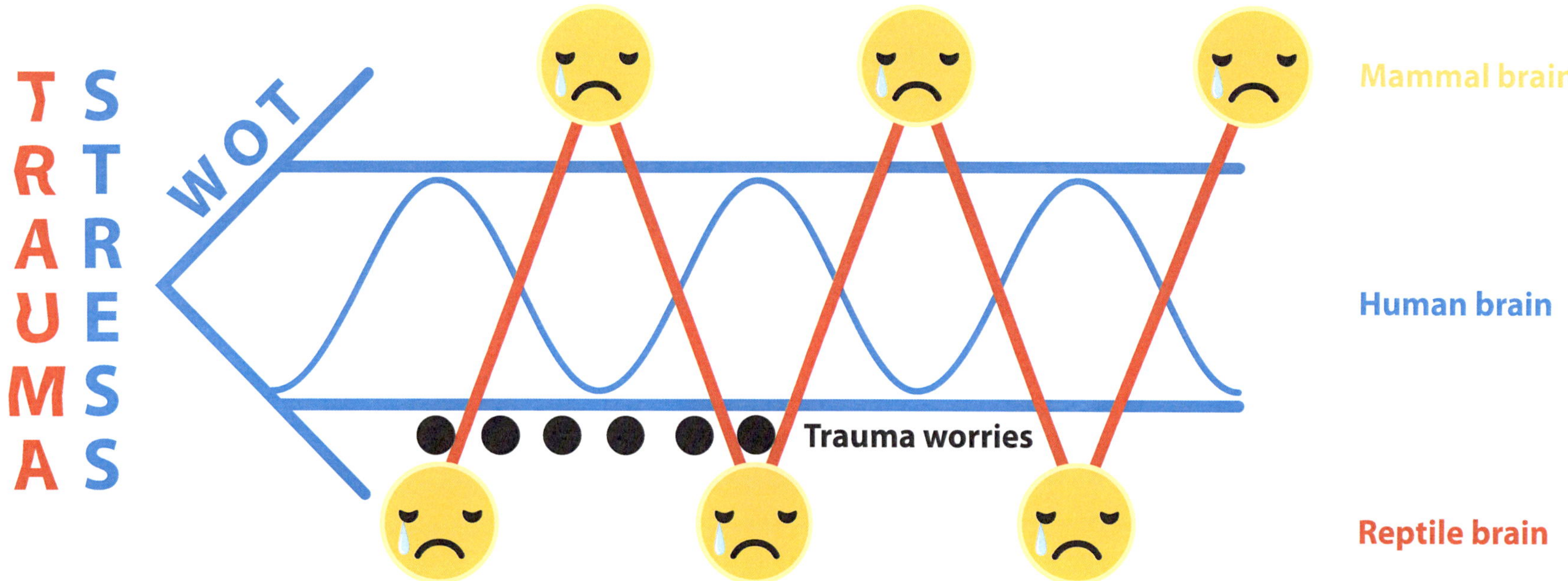

Trauma worries

- Parents fighting, hitting, shouting
- Bullying
- Home alone
- No safe place to sleep
- Unsafe touching
- Not enough food
- Changing houses and schools a lot
- Adults drinking or taking drugs

It can take 15 to 20 minutes to come back inside my window and because my human brain is switched off, it is not a good time to talk to me about things before then. I can't concentrate, focus or remember very well. I can't make sense of conversation or take it in, so I may withdraw or lash out.

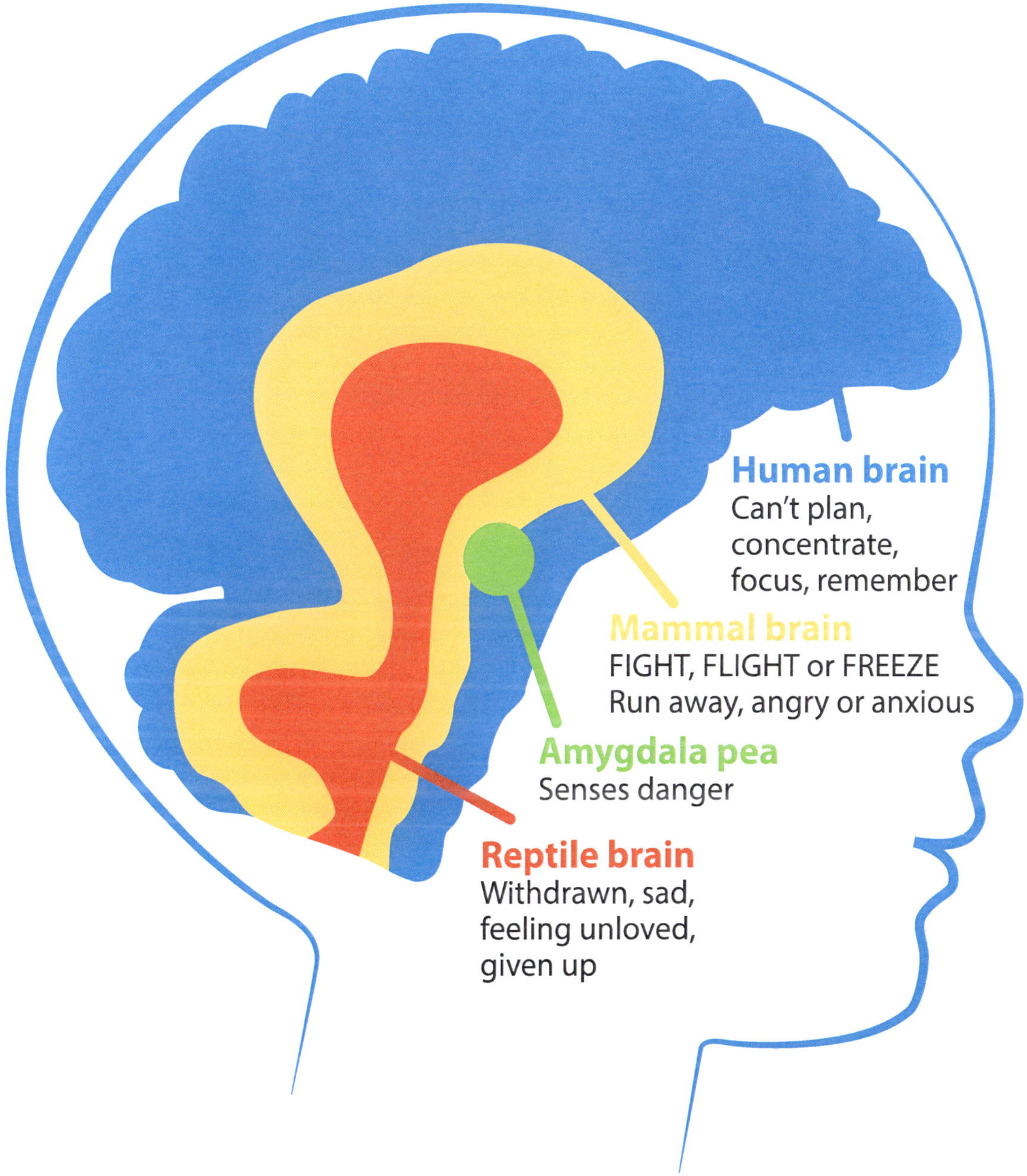

Things that help me come inside my window

- Safety and a calm quiet place
- Sleep
- Food and drink
- Exercise like walking, running, scooting or biking
- Music
- Mindfulness breathing
- A safe person to talk to

Bibliography

Corrigan, F., Fisher, J., and Nutt, D. (2011). 'Autonomic dysregulation and the Window of Tolerance model of the effects of complex emotional trauma', *Journal of Psychopharmacology*, 25(1), 17–25. https://doi.org/10.1177/0269881109354930

Felitti, V. J., Anda, R. F., Nordenberg, D., Williamson, D. F., Spitz, A.M., Edwards, V., … Perma-Nente, K. (1998). 'Relationship of childhood abuse and household dysfunction to many of the leading causes of death in adults: the Adverse Childhood Experiences (ACE) Study', *Am J Prev Med*, 14. Retrieved from www.elsevier.com

Ogden, P., Pain, C., and Fisher, J. (n.d.). A Sensorimotor Approach to the Treatment of Trauma and Dissociation. http://doi.org/10.1016/j.psc.2005.10.012

Siegel, D.J. (1999), *The Developing Mind*. New York: Guilford Press.

Struik, A. (2014). *Treating Chronically Traumatised Children*. Sussex: Routledge.

Van der Kolk B.A. (1996) 'The body keeps the score: approaches to the psychobiology of posttraumatic stress disorder'. In: *Traumatic Stress: The Effects of Overwhelming Experience on Mind, Body, and Society*. New York: Guilford Press, 214–241.

Acknowledgements

I wish to thank all the professionals who have shared their knowledge of trauma therapy work in many forms. I am humbled by your work and am constantly deepening my knowledge of its application.

www.ingramcontent.com/pod-product-compliance
Ingram Content Group UK Ltd.
Pitfield, Milton Keynes, MK11 3LW, UK
UKRC032309290726
14090UKWH00004B/407

* 9 7 8 0 4 7 3 4 8 2 6 8 8 *